ALL ABOUT ANXIETY

by Carrie Lewis

illustrated by
Sophia Touliatou

beaming books
MINNEAPOLIS

CHAPTER 1
WHAT IS ANXIETY?

Hello, Anxiety. Let's get to know each other!

People talk about anxiety all the time, but what do you think anxiety really is? What does it feel like?

Is anxiety those butterflies you get in your stomach before taking a test? Is it that nagging doubt you might have about whether or not you are popular with your friends? Or is anxiety the same as being afraid—afraid of the dark or afraid of strangers?

The truth is that many feelings can be called anxiety, and many things can cause anxiety for different people. Sometimes anxiety might feel like fear of a particular thing. Sometimes it might be vaguer: a little voice in your head telling you that something is going to go wrong.

To feel some anxiety is normal and even healthy. It helps us to be on our guard in particularly dangerous situations. It also helps us to perform at our best on tests and in other stressful situations.

One thing is for sure: EVERYBODY feels anxiety. So when do we know that anxiety has stopped being normal and become a problem?

If you need to see a doctor about anxiety, that's usually because it has become a problem in your life. This might be because anxiety is stopping you from enjoying your life and doing things you would like to do. The worry might have become overwhelming and started to take up a lot of your time. Or maybe other people have noticed that you are behaving in an unusual way, or that you are unhappy.

We'll get to know anxiety throughout this book—as well as some ways to address anxiety and live with anxiety. Read on and see what you recognize from your own life.

A Few Types of Anxiety

These are some of the most common types of anxiety that have been identified by experts. You might know people who have some of these. You might have even felt some of them yourself.

Generalized anxiety

This is when you feel that things are going to go wrong or that bad things will happen almost all the time, whether or not there is a good reason to be anxious. Sometimes it comes with other problems like sleeping poorly or restlessness, or with physical problems like an upset stomach or headaches. Some people with generalized anxiety find it hard to concentrate and are easily distracted.

Social anxiety

Often this type of anxiety makes you appear shy or self-conscious to other people. If you have ever felt awkward about answering a question in front of everyone in your class or about having to stand and talk in front of the school, you might know what this feels like. Someone who has social anxiety might feel worried about meeting new people, but they might even feel worried in everyday social situations like talking to friends and people they know well. They might often feel that they will say the "wrong" thing.

Phobias

A phobia is an extreme fear of a specific thing, such as spiders (arachnophobia) or mice (musophobia), or situations such as heights (acrophobia) or small spaces (claustrophobia). Many people are a little afraid of these things, but a serious phobia is one that gets in the way of everyday life and affects the decisions you make. If you can't use an elevator, then your claustrophobia is an obstacle.

Panic Attacks

This is when someone feels frightened suddenly or for no obvious reason. They can have a racing heart, dizziness, or trouble breathing. It might be that the person has been generally anxious or worried about something else before this happens.

Obsessive-compulsive Disorder

Or OCD for short. When people talk about someone being "OCD," they often think of someone who has lots of obsessive habits, like handwashing or tidying. But this isn't the only way that Obsessive-Compulsive Disorder shows itself. Some people with OCD believe that something terrible will happen if they don't follow a particular routine or pattern of behavior. An example might be that if the sufferer doesn't put their clothes on in a particular order every day, they think they will be in an accident. Sometimes they might also worry about forgetting things and start to overplan or feel panicked about small details that seem wrong to them.

Separation anxiety

Some people find being apart from their loved ones frightening. They can't help themselves from imagining that something bad will happen to the person they love while they are apart. This can be a problem for parents and children, especially when parents start a new job or children start a new school.

It is possible to have more than one type of anxiety. What is important is that you decide how much anxiety you feel, or whether it is getting in the way of your life. If you feel that it is, the advice throughout this book will show you what you can do. Of course, talking to an adult is always a good place to start.

One thing is for sure: you can do things to reduce unhelpful anxiety. Later on, we will talk about the techniques, methods, exercises, and therapies you can try, with or without other people. Don't brush your feelings aside. Just like everyone else, you have a right to experience well-being and to enjoy your own life.

ENJOY LIFE!

Is this anxiety normal?

You might think that some types of anxiety are more justified than others. For example, being anxious before an exam is more justified than being anxious because you saw a mouse in the loft.

Right?

Not quite! Every type of anxiety is normal because that's the way that our brain tells us that there's a problem. Sometimes, though, a bad experience in the past, or an underlying phobia or anxiety, can make a problem seem bigger than it really is. Because of that, our anxieties can seem strange to other people.

Here is a story about two sisters who are anxious about different things.

Jane and her sister Zara both suffer from anxiety about particular things. Jane is afraid of taking tests but Zara is afraid of spiders. Jane teases Zara about her phobia of spiders:

"Who ever heard of a spider doing you any harm? Unless it's a spider wearing boots and carrying an axe . . . and I've never seen one of those!"

Zara answers, "But what about you and your fear of taking tests? You always study hard and do well in the end."

Then Jane replies, "You can't possibly compare my fear of tests with a fear of spiders. There's no similarity! I could really fail sometimes! But there are no poisonous spiders around here. These spiders never hurt anyone. Except flies."

who is right?

Well, you might say that both of them are equally right and wrong.

To Jane and Zara, these fears are very real. Most spiders do not pose a danger to people. And doing badly on a test isn't something to worry about, as long as you study and do your best. However, to Jane and Zara, the fear of these things has become much bigger than the real threat. Something in both Jane's and Zara's memories or experiences has made them feel that tests and spiders are more threatening than they really are.

The important thing is not whether a fear or anxiety is "right" or "wrong." It's all about whether the anxiety is starting to affect your life negatively!

Anxiety—get real!

One way for Jane and Zara to get their anxiety back under control might be to think about how small the real risks are, and to look at why they became anxious about these things in the first place.

For some people, their fear of some things feels like a spiral: it grows and grows as one fear leads to another, and another, and another. Slight worry about how you will perform on one test can spiral into a deep fear about how you will succeed on all tests and even in your future career. Learning to see when you are making this "spiraling" happen can help you to control it and not to react this way in future.

So is there any sort of fear that isn't "normal"?

Not really. All fear is real to the person who feels it, and it's not helpful to tease or shame people who suffer from fears or phobias.

There are, however, ways that we can start to see our fears for what they really are: an echo of something we once saw or heard that made us afraid at the time.

Some counselors and therapists specialize in techniques that help you to alter the way you think about these things. You can learn methods that can reprogram your thoughts so that your reactions to particular things become less extreme. We'll talk about these techniques in more detail later in the book.

Anxiety—all in your imagination?

The imagination is a wonderful thing. With our imaginations, we can explore made-up worlds or make up stories to entertain ourselves and others. We can use our imaginations in the form of empathy to understand other people and sympathize with them. You might have been praised for having a "vivid" imagination when you have written a story, painted a picture, or come up with an original idea.

When it comes to anxiety, however, the imagination can be less friendly. Our imagination can make us believe that ordinary, everyday events are threatening. It can make threats appear to us simply out of nowhere. Nighttime can be an especially tricky time for anxiety and the imagination.

Fear of the dark

First of all, there's the fear of darkness— and before you think that this is a silly, childish phase that we grow out of, think again. Your prehistoric ancestors had to keep their senses alert in the darkness to hear when dangerous creatures were approaching. If they woke in the night imagining that a creature like a saber-toothed tiger was about to pounce on them, they were probably right!

So if, when you were younger, you didn't want to turn the light out in case there was a goblin—or a saber-toothed tiger—under the bed, then this was just your prehistoric senses keeping watch as you rested.

Don't be too hard on yourself if you still feel some fear of the dark even as you get older—it may mean that you still feel some of your prehistoric ancestors' fears. If this is a particular problem for you, however, try to remember that your instincts are tricking you. The fear is not real: there are no wild animals in your bedroom, and a creak outside your door is more likely to be the furnace switching off than something dangerous (unless you have a brother or sister in there who is a particularly bad snorer, but even then they won't pounce—probably).

Top Tip!

To reduce or stop anxiety and insomnia, try writing down anything that makes you anxious before you go to bed. This can help you step back and keep anxiety in perspective. You could also try some relaxation techniques once you get into bed. We will look at these in more detail in chapter 5.

Insomnia — or when you can't sleep

Another problem that happens at night is insomnia, and this can be particularly tricky if you suffer from anxiety.

Nighttime is when we are meant to rest, but for someone who is anxious, the lack of distractions and things to keep us busy can give our worries extra room to grow. When we should be sleeping, we are turning problems over and over in our minds until they make us feel anxious.

This happens for the same reasons as fear of the dark. When we are trying to rest, our instincts for danger may remain alert. For people who worry at night, this instinctive fear of danger feeds into normal, everyday concerns and makes them seem much, much bigger than they are.

what do I call *this* feeling?

There are lots of names for some of the bad feelings we have. In this book, we're talking about anxiety, but here are other words for what we might be experiencing, and what they might mean.

Depression

Depression is a medical condition that affects the sufferer's mood and behavior, and that may require the person who has it to see a doctor. Often someone suffering from depression has a very low mood and finds it difficult to manage everyday life. Not everyone with depression will show their symptoms in the same way, but one common symptom is a loss of interest in relationships or in activities that usually bring enjoyment. Often the person also feels tired and wants to sleep a lot, but has trouble sleeping at night. You might not be able to see depression on the outside, but that doesn't mean that you or someone else isn't feeling it on the inside. Depression can co-occur with other disorders like anxiety.

Paranoia

When someone suffers from paranoia, they may believe that they are always being watched, or that people are talking about them. People often use the word in a more common way if they think someone is making too much of a situation: "Tom's really paranoid about getting home late." But when paranoia is very serious, it may be an indication of a serious mental disorder. Again, it's all about whether paranoia affects your life negatively.

Worry

Worry is a word we often use to talk about a particular thing we are bothered by and that we keep thinking about constantly. If someone worries a lot about all sorts of things, that might be a sign that they have more general anxiety. However, it is normal and healthy to worry sometimes. Worrying about an upcoming event or test results, or even things in your family, is bound to happen from time to time. As long as it comes and goes, this is fine. But if worry persists, then it could be an indication of a more serious problem.

stress

We use the word *stress* to mean that we feel there is too much to do or too much to think about. If you have a lot of homework you may feel stressed about doing it all, or you might feel there is a lot to think about when you experience a major life event, like changing schools or moving to a new home. A little stress is okay—it can help you focus and work hard on difficult things. But if stress becomes a regular part of your everyday life and starts affecting you negatively, it might be time to think about ways to cut back on the stress in your life, as stress can easily lead to persistent anxiety.

CHAPTER 2
WHAT MAKES YOU ANXIOUS?

"where does my anxiety come from?"

This is a tricky question to answer and will vary from one person to another.

Our parents

There is some evidence that genes passed down from parents to children may make us more (or less) sensitive to different types of fear or danger. If your parents are anxious, this doesn't mean you will be anxious, but genes might slightly increase the chance that you will experience anxiety. You might have also learned anxious behavior from observing an anxious parent.

memories of frightening experiences

YAP!

Feelings of anxiety can also start with some sort of frightening experience that happened to you in the past. Anything that reminds you of this first experience may make you feel frightened in the same way. For example, if a dog bit you or scared you by barking when you were little, you may grow up with a fear of dogs. That's because your brain has learned to associate dogs with a threat.

other people's frightening experiences

Sometimes, parents and older adults accidentally teach children to be afraid of the things that they are afraid of. For example, if your grandma is so afraid of spiders that she always asks your grandpa to put them in the garden, you may have learned to see spiders as scary. That doesn't mean that spiders are dangerous—or even frightening. Probably, your grandma also saw her grandma ask her grandpa to put spiders in the garden, and she has accidentally carried on this fear and given it to you.

where does my anxiety come from?

Growing up in difficult circumstances

Sometimes, the situation we grow up in can cause us to feel anxious in lots of different ways. If as a child you have a close relative with a long-term illness, or you lose your home and suddenly have to move, this can lead to some types of anxiety as you get older. You may fear losing people you love if you have lost someone close to you, or you may worry that there is never enough money if you have grown up in a home where money was tight. You may grow up with a fear of change if, as a child, unwanted change is forced on you. If the environment you grow up in is stressful or unsafe, you may experience anxiety because you feel as though you always have to be on alert.

If you grew up in a situation that caused you anxiety, or if you're in an anxiety-creating situation right now, please don't blame yourself. The circumstances that surround you are not your fault. The most important thing is for you to take care of yourself and change your circumstances if necessary. If you are currently in danger or live in a circumstance that is not safe or healthy for you, please reach out to a friend or trusted adult for help. Check the resources at the end of this book for some ideas for how to get help.

Remember!

If you experience anxiety for any of these reasons, it can be really tempting to get mad at yourself or feel ashamed—ashamed of your anxious genes, the scary experiences that have taught you to be anxious, or your life circumstances. Try not to do that. Whatever the reason for it, your anxiety is not your fault. Be kind to yourself, take care of yourself, and take steps to address your anxiety. You'll learn more about that as the book goes on. For now, we'll move on to trying to understand what's going on in your brain—and your body—when you feel anxiety.

Is my anxiety caused by chemicals in my brain?

Although it might not always feel like it, your brain is full of activity all the time. This is the result of chemicals called **neurotransmitters**. These neurotransmitters carry information between the cells in your brain every millisecond of every day. There are several different neurotransmitters, but some of them have been specifically linked to our moods and emotions. These are **serotonin**, **dopamine,** and **norepinephrine**.

Some researchers believe that low levels of these neurotransmitters, especially serotonin, are a cause of anxiety and other disorders, such as depression. These researchers have suggested that increasing the levels of these neurotransmitters in the brain could help people feel better.

Medication for anxiety is intended to raise the levels of neurotransmitters in the brain, and the improvement seen in patients after using this medication is evidence of the relationship between neurotransmitters and anxiety. Medication can be very effective for some people!

However, medication isn't always the answer. Research suggests that medication helps around six out of ten patients. That's a lot of people, but it's not everybody. There definitely seems to be a link between neurotransmitters and mood problems like anxiety and depression—but it's a complicated relationship, and we don't fully understand it yet.

If you experience anxiety and think that chemicals in your brain might be to blame, the most important thing is to talk to a therapist, counselor, or doctor. These people will consider your symptoms and help you to understand whether you might be a good candidate for anxiety medication, or whether it might be better to try some other method of addressing your anxiety first. There are other things you can do—like exercise or eating a healthy diet— that can help you send more happy neurotransmitters like dopamine to your brain, without any pills!

norepinephrine

dopamine

SYNAPSE

seratonin

How do neurotransmitters work?

When one brain cell needs to send a signal to another brain cell, it will release neurotransmitters. These neurotransmitters then cross the synapse (that's the space between two brain cells) and trigger another brain cell. That brain cell may then release its own neurotransmitters, which cross another synapse and trigger another brain cell . . . and so on, communicating in a complex way across your whole brain.

Anxiety: what's really going on in your body?

When we feel anxiety, our bodies may start to show certain symptoms. These may include:

INCREASED HEART RATE

RAPID BREATHING AND SWEATING

UPSET STOMACH AND A PANICKY FEELING

AN URGE TO RUN AWAY!

These symptoms tell us a lot. They tell us that our body is reacting the way it has been programmed to react since prehistoric times. The part of the brain that produces anxiety is located deep in the brain, in the part that's been there since early stages in our evolution! To understand what anxiety is all about, we need to know what kinds of things used to make our ancestors anxious back in the days of early *Homo sapiens*—the first humans who ever walked the earth.

Before we had laptops, mobile phones, grocery stores, and safe, warm houses with heating and indoor plumbing, humans were in a constant battle to survive in the wild. Early humans had to deal with extreme weather, natural disasters, and wild animals. One part of the human brain evolved brilliantly to deal with these kinds of serious threats. This part of the brain is called the **amygdala**.

The **amygdala** is located just here in your brain.

It is trained to deal with **mortal danger**, which means danger that can **kill you**.

Top Tip!

Sometimes when you feel anxiety, your brain is actually overreacting and making your body behave as if there's something that's trying to actually kill you. Your brain doesn't understand movies, text messages, homework, or social media. It doesn't have the ability to differentiate between a big threat and a small threat, so when it reacts to a scary part of a movie, or an upsetting social media post, or a really stressful test at school, your brain can make your body react as if it is in mortal danger.

In the past, if an early human was attacked by a wild animal, or another early human, the amygdala would swing into action, triggering a response to either confront and destroy the threat **(fight)**, or otherwise to run in the opposite direction **(flight)**.

Fight!

Flight!

This **"fight or flight"** reaction was essential to the success of early humans in a dangerous world. By producing an immediate, powerful emotional response, the amygdala gave humans enough of an instant kick of adrenaline to deal with the danger.

However, what's useful when you are called on to fight a saber-toothed tiger or a wild boar is less useful in some situations we face today. For example, if someone texts you to say they don't want to go to the movies on Tuesday, it is not a mortal threat. No one's life is in danger! But if your amygdala gets wind that you are facing a threat to your self-confidence, and maybe feeling rejected by your "herd," it might go into overdrive and start to trigger some of the bigger "fight or flight" reactions, perhaps making you want to yell and shout at that person (fight) or run away and hide (flight).

Try This!

If you are facing something that makes you feel anxious, try to get your amygdala under control. Take some deep breaths and try to see the "threat" for what it is, and not how your amygdala sees it. A test is not a mortal threat—it is a piece of paper, and even though a bad grade won't feel good, it won't kill you. A tricky moment in a friendship can be repaired by sharing a donut—it won't end your days on the planet.

CHAPTER 3
YOUR INNER ZOO AND ZOOKEEPER

Anxiety—it's like a zoo!

Next, we're going to explore in a bit more detail some of the real fears we face in life. Why do they trigger our amygdala and cause us anxiety? Is this okay or not, and can we control it?

Not everything in this chapter will be something that you have experienced yourself, but some of it may seem a bit familiar. First, here's a story.

A day at the zoo

It's six o'clock in the morning when Fred the zookeeper arrives for work. He looks after all the animals in the zoo, and they are a wild bunch. The zebras run around without stopping, the parrots chatter endlessly, and the snakes seem to disappear, only to rear up and hiss, ready to pounce, when you least expect them. Then there are the mischievous monkeys swinging around and playing tricks on each other.

The animals seem difficult to control, but Fred doesn't mind them because he knows what they need. He gives the snakes plenty of shade so that they can sleep, he gives the monkeys new toys to play with, and he makes sure that the zebras have soft grass to lie down in. He takes anything too noisy or frightening further away so that the animals can relax. Lastly, he gives the parrots more room to fly and plenty of juicy insects and fruit to eat. The animals settle down and spend the day peacefully playing and entertaining the visitors.

so what's this got to do with anxiety?

In some ways an anxious mind is like a zoo. Some thoughts run out of control (like the zebras), some thoughts are "noisy" and won't go away (like the parrots), some thoughts play tricks on you (like the monkeys), and some can seem threatening (like the snakes). But as Fred knows, if you treat your thoughts and feelings properly, you can help them settle down so they don't run wild and destroy the entire zoo (your mind)!

Around 20 percent of the population is thought to be genetically more sensitive to anxiety than the rest. If you feel you are part of the 20 percent, you may need to work a little harder on your "calm" routines, but taking control of anxiety is still within your reach.

Friend or enemy?

Your amygdala is a bit like a zoo animal—it's not really bad: it just needs managing. When it's under control, the amygdala is a friend because it helps you stay alert to possible danger. If you control it, then it can help you deal with difficult situations: the adrenaline kick that comes from your amygdala, whether it's before a math test or while you're doing a tricky stunt on your skateboard, can help you to concentrate better and be more alert. It can encourage you to learn more by engaging your curiosity, and it can improve your overall performance in something by alerting you to challenges.

It's only when the amygdala gets out of control and makes you anxious about things that aren't really threatening, or makes you anxious all the time, that it becomes your enemy.

The news

Sometimes it's hard to avoid seeing or hearing about things on the news that make us afraid or anxious. After all, real life involves some pretty serious and daunting issues.

The news constantly informs us about the following:

- People dying or getting hurt. News about terrible events like school shootings can seem particularly upsetting because they affect people we can easily relate to.

- Problems with the climate and how this might affect the future of our planet with floods and higher temperatures.

- War, and countries arguing in a way that looks as if it might end in war.

- People suffering from illnesses like cancer and HIV.

These things might seem particularly frightening because they are far beyond our own control.

It can feel as if we are being dragged along with no say in what's happening to our future.

However out of control this might make you feel, it is possible to put these feelings to good use. You can't cure the world on your own—but there are some things you can do that might make you feel better and help make the world a little better too. They might make you feel as if you are taking a little bit of control. Feeling some worry about the world is understandable. But by doing something—even something small—to help the situation, you are taking control. That helps the world *and* your anxiety.

So how about this? If you feel worried by something that you see on the news, take some small action to make it better.

Things you can do!

Try to understand what's going on with the climate, and do the things that you can: **recycle, buy less stuff, use less energy.**

In politics, learn who has the kind of policies that make the world a better place and support them. As a kid, you can't vote yet—but you still have a voice. You can combine forces with other kids and make the adults take notice. You are not powerless, and you have the right to have a say in your own future!

It's also okay to just turn off the news and take a break from all the problems of the world for a while. It's important to do what you can to try to make the world a better place—but you are not responsible for fixing the world. Take a break. Do something that's fun, something that makes you happy.

Fiction

It's not necessarily a bad thing to feel anxious about things you see in books, movies, or TV shows. People who write made-up stories want to make you a little anxious: it's called suspense and conflict. A little bit of anxiety while watching an exciting movie can be part of the fun!

But people's imaginations behave very differently when it comes to fiction. Some people can separate real things from imaginary things quite easily. Some people, however, are more sensitive to things they see in fiction, because they echo or remind them of something from real life.

Here's a story:

Jake and Joe watch a TV show where the main character is captured by some villains and is tied up in a cellar with a blindfold on his eyes. Joe is unaffected: he knows it's pretend. Jake, however, can't watch, and then later can't get the scary situation out of his head. Jake knows that in real life someone in the situation of the show's main character would have been very frightened. Although the people are make-believe, the fear and pain are real to Jake.

Know yourself—and remember your inner zookeeper

If you are one of those people who is affected by fiction on TV or online, here are two top tips:

1. Avoid things that may upset you. Remember how Fred the zookeeper took the frightening things farther away so that the animals would calm down? That's what you can do. If a TV show is really scaring you, you can switch it off. If a book is upsetting you, put it away for a while. And if your friends like scary movies but you don't, have some distractions at hand, like a tablet, game, or book, so you can take a break during the nasty bits without feeling embarrassed.

2. Understand that the fear you are feeling probably says some good things about you. You are sensitive and aware of the emotions of others. You have empathy and sympathy for the things you see around you.

No one is wrong.

Joe and Jake are just experiencing the suspense of the TV show in a different way. Joe is enjoying the story as make-believe. But the story is triggering a real fear or anxiety for Jake. To him, it doesn't feel made up.

Hormones!

One common cause of anxiety in young people is the changes that are going on in their brains and bodies.

You have probably heard about some of the changes that happen to your body when you go through puberty, like growth spurts, body hair, and acne. You may be less aware of how puberty affects your brain.

During puberty, the brain grows at its fastest rate since you were a toddler. Your new, larger brain will be more under the control of the **limbic** system (that's the emotional bit) than a grown-up's. Over time, the **prefrontal cortex** (that's the bit at the front of the brain that tries to keep some order) grows and brings the emotions a bit more under the control of logic and reasonable thought. But until the prefrontal cortex catches up, this might make teenage you react very emotionally.

sorry about that.
It's your brain's fault!

Other changes that come as your brain grows make you more aware of how you appear to other people. This can lead you to feel self-conscious and as if everyone is watching you. When a teenager becomes obsessed with creating the perfect hairstyle or taking endless selfies, this is mainly because they are hyper-aware of the way they look to other people. Luckily, this will pass. (Well, mostly—adults can be pretty aware of their appearance too!)

Look after yourself

Because the changes in your head can't be seen, it's easy to underestimate them. The emotional rollercoaster that you go through in puberty can make you angrier than usual, more shy than usual, and more unsure of yourself. All of this can make you anxious as you adjust to the "new you." To get through all this in one piece, spend time with people who treat you with kindness and understanding and let you be yourself. Remember that you're doing your best and that some emotional outbursts are a natural part of this stage in your life. Eat well, exercise, get plenty of sleep, and remember that it will all settle down soon.

changing family

Family can be a source of joy or a source of stress and anxiety, and most people experience both of these extremes.

Family changes can make you particularly anxious. In the list below are some kinds that might make you anxious.

separation and divorce

It's very common for parents to divorce or separate, but the effects on each family will be different and always difficult. When children see their parents separate, their relationships to their parents change:

- One parent may be absent.

- Both parents may be angrier or unhappier than usual.

- New families may be formed with stepbrothers and sisters, creating new relationships in your own home.

This kind of change is very difficult because so many emotions are involved: anger, sadness, and uncertainty, just for a start.

Death in the family

The death of someone in or close to your family may affect you and those around you at the same time. It can take families a long time to deal with losing someone, and grief can go on for years. This is completely normal. Try to accept it if people around you are sad, and be honest about your own feelings of loss. Don't sweep them away. Remember and cherish the person you have lost.

A new baby

"Aren't you lucky having a new baby sister to play with?" Well, that's not always how it feels. Suddenly your parents aren't your own anymore and no one's getting any sleep. You might even find yourself being part of the backup team of diaper changers when your mom or dad needs a break. Although it will not be what anyone else thinks, you might suddenly feel as if you are second-best or, even worse, that you have been replaced. Try to accept the new relationship that's come into your life—as the new baby gets bigger they will most likely think that you are awesome!

Keep reminding yourself that the worst changes are only temporary and better things are coming.

Job loss or money worry

Very often, parents and other grown-ups go through times when they worry about money. This might be because they have changed jobs or got laid off, or it might be because they have had to find extra money to pay for something like medical bills or a change to the house. Hopefully, worries like this come and go, but when they come they can put a strain on the whole household.

When an adult loses a job, they become uncertain not only about how they will continue to earn money, but also about where their future will take them. This uncertainty can lead adults to feel very unhappy and confused. They may seem angrier and more irritable than usual.

If you hear parents saying "We can't afford that at the moment" about small treats or new things, do your best to go along with it without worrying too much. Almost all families have some ups and downs with jobs and money. Just because money is tight right now doesn't mean that it will be forever. Focus on the good things you do have rather than on the nice things you can't have right now. Gratitude is a great way to short-circuit money anxiety.

Moving to a different house or city

Whether you move because a parent has changed jobs, your parents have separated, or any other reason, moving to a new place can be very unsettling. Moving can be even worse if you have to change schools as well. Having to fit in with a new group of friends or leave behind places that are comfortable and familiar in order to "start again" can lead to some complicated reactions in your head. You may find yourself wondering, "Who am I?" as your sense of who you are is often tied up in your surroundings.

Remember to give yourself time. Things will feel strange at the start, but time is a healer and will tend to make things better after a little while. Instead of regretting what you have left behind, look forward to the exciting things you can now discover.

Finding help—because sometimes your inner zookeeper takes time off

Need help? If any of these anxiety-creating circumstances feel overwhelming, there might be someone in school who can help you through it. Many schools have a counselor or a specially trained teacher to help children go through big changes. Some schools might even let you talk to an older child who has had similar experiences. In any case, talking to someone you trust outside the family might be a big help. If you don't want to talk to someone at school, try a grandparent or a family friend. Always remember, changes like this can be very challenging, but the effects don't last forever.

The pressure to succeed

Sometimes in life, it can feel as if you only get noticed when you're the best. There's constant pressure to succeed and to show everyone else that you're succeeding. Social media is full of people showing off their latest prize or achievement, or the amazing time they're having with their friends. Sometimes we see people going on and on about the fantastic new gadget or clothes they have bought because they or their family are so super-amazingly rich and successful.

Whatever type of success you are looking for, whether it's friends, money, or school prizes, it's likely that looking for it will cause a certain amount of anxiety. For example, if popularity is how you want to be successful, you might feel as if you have failed when a friendship ends or someone else is more popular than you. If you are always top of the class and ace every test, it may come as a shock when someone else beats your score—and one day that is sure to happen.

While a little bit of worry can motivate us to do our best, sometimes we feel like our worry guarantees that we will perform well. However, often we would have succeeded even if we didn't worry so much. You can start by worrying 20 percent less and trusting you'll get the same results.

Remember, success and failure often aren't really that big a deal. They come and go, and something else comes along.

Instead of thinking about success, think about how you got to where you are—and remember to be proud of yourself for ALL that you have achieved— the parts that people see and the parts that they don't.

consider these:

- What have you learned?

- What have you done well?

- How have you helped someone else?

- Did you make the best effort that you could have made?

- What would you do differently next time?

temporoparietal lobe

Answers to these questions may be where your true success in life lies. If you made your friend happy for a day, or you tried harder than you've ever tried before, that counts! These aren't things you can post all over social media, and they may not get you to the top step of the prize podium, but they are still real. They still mean that you did well.

If you want to succeed in something, then consider kindness. Acts of kindness stimulate the **temporoparietal lobe** in the brain, which can make you happier and healthier.

Top Tip!

Instead of counting your friends, try to be a better friend to everyone. Instead of relying on your natural brainy brilliance, try to learn a new skill or teach someone else how to do something that they find difficult. These are great ways to live a successful life and will make you feel good about yourself too. You don't have to measure your success at all. Trying to make the world a better place will bring benefits to everyone—even if it doesn't appear on social media.

comparing myself

So, you're doing okay. You've got some good friends and school could be worse. But then your best friend/worst enemy/big sister/little brother is always doing better than you! It's either your grades at school, or having the cooler friends, or having a really great fashion style that you never seem to be able to copy.

Top Tip!
Be grateful for who you are!

For everything you envy in someone else, there will be something you do have that is really great! Every time you find yourself comparing yourself negatively with others, sit down and start making a list of everything that's great about *you*.

Comparing yourself with other people is likely to lead to anxiety about yourself, and it also risks spoiling your relationships with other people. If your best friend has the sparkling blue eyes that you have always longed to have, or your little sister can run the fastest hundred meters in the school, that can hurt. It's hard when other people have the things that you want.

When you start to compare yourself negatively with other people, it can make you lose sight of your own gifts. When you are desperate to be valued by those around you, you imagine a threat to your position because of the area in which you are overshadowed. This is a false fear—an unruly zoo animal—that you need to learn to tame. You are a whole person with your own unique strengths and areas in which you excel. No one can ever replace you because you're the only you that exists! When people see you for who you are, they see all of you—the marvelous parts too.

Getting out of the comparison game and feeling grateful for who you are can ease your anxiety and also keep your relationships in better shape.

The way I look

As we get older and go through puberty, we are sometimes hyper-aware of the way we look to other people, and we may become very self-conscious in public. We may also become aware of how many images there are of good-looking men and women on screens and advertisements all the time.

It can be very easy to start thinking that the attractive people you see in films and in ads look the "right" way. You may even start to think that you should do whatever you can to look just like them. You might start by doing your hair like them, then wearing the same sort of clothes, and before you know it, you're a look-alike!

You may become so convinced that this person looks "right" that you might start to be too critical of your own appearance, and this can be quite dangerous to your self-esteem and a cause of anxiety. You might feel that your curly hair will never look as shiny as your idol's glossy, straight hair, but that doesn't mean your hair is wrong—it's nice in its own way.

Top Tip!
Everyone's body is good

Ads and movies are full of people who seem perfect, but that doesn't mean that there's anything wrong with the way you look. There are lots of different ways of looking good. Staying healthy in your body and mind and remaining confident are the best ways to look and feel good.

And bodies are about more than their looks! To flip your anxious thoughts about your looks, try to think about what your body can do. Your strong and graceful body can do sports. Your hands can make things. Your brain contains your thoughts and your unique point of view—it makes you you. Doing things you love with your body can be a great boost to your self-esteem and body image.

other people

Most people, if they are honest with themselves, probably feel afraid of other people at one time or another. This might be a fear of a particular teacher or someone else at school, like a bully. It could be someone who makes you feel small either on purpose or by accident.

We all want to be liked, don't we? It might be that we want to be liked for our skills or knowledge, or we might want people to see us as likeable or popular. And then there's appearance: most people want other people to like the way they look.

This is another thing that goes back to our early human instincts! Our earliest ancestors were more likely to survive in packs or groups. A human who was rejected by their group would be unlikely to survive in the wild alone. This meant that fitting in, or not being rejected by the "herd," was vital to survival. Our instincts today often carry this into modern life as a desire to be accepted or liked by as many people as possible. When someone is mean to us, this is why it really seems to hurt—our brain interprets it as a threat to our very survival!

So, going back to the amygdala, we know that the fear that we feel of rejection or ridicule is often an echo of the primitive part of our brains. It's important to remember, however, that wearing clothes or makeup that have gone a bit out of fashion, not having the latest phone, or even being teased by the school bully are unlikely to result in your family or your friends driving you out into the cold on a snowy night. Your survival is not necessarily at stake.

If you feel constantly afraid of being rejected or judged by other people, try to remember that you might have no real reason to fear. Often it is just your brain's primitive fear of rejection by the herd getting a bit out of hand. Focus instead on the community and support system you do have, the people who accept, love, and support you exactly the way you are.

However, if someone really is threatening your physical safety or mental well-being, you should absolutely take your feelings of fear and anxiety seriously. You might meet some people in life who do want to threaten and intimidate you. If this happens, it is really important to remember that they have the problem, not you. Talk to someone. Reach out to a friend or trusted adult. Get help to put yourself in a safe situation. This is one of those cases when your anxiety is your friend—it's telling you that something really is wrong!

People who don't help me feel my best

Some people in our lives are better for us than others. While some people make us feel our very best, other people can leave us with a sinking feeling for no obvious reason. This is true throughout our lives. Friends who don't let us feel our best can be a great cause of anxiety—whether they cause anxiety in the first place or make our existing anxiety worse.

Anxiety-causing friendships show themselves in different ways.

Possessive friends

Ever had a friend who wanted to shower you with attention, but got angry when you spent time with other friends or spent time doing what they didn't want to do? This is possessiveness. A possessive friend like this mainly wants you around for their own benefit—not for a real two-way friendship. Sticking around with a friend like this might make you feel anxious because you are not living up to what someone else wants you to be. Whether or not you want to hold on to the friendship, make sure you stand up for yourself and keep doing the things that you want to do.

You look better in that dress than in the one you wore yesterday.

Negative friends

Another type of friend who might make you feel uncomfortable is one who says things that make you feel bad about yourself or who puts you down a lot. These are negative friends. Have a look at what the two friends are saying on this page.

The first sentence seems to be a compliment, but it also includes a suggestion that you didn't look good yesterday for no obvious reason. The second sentence, however, is completely positive.

A sentence on its own isn't enough to judge a friendship on, but if you have a friend or friends who say things like Friend A often, or friends who talk about themselves and never ask about you, or who put down or mock your choices or the things you like, then they can cause you to doubt yourself and lose confidence, which could contribute to feelings of social anxiety or generalized anxiety.

Top Tip!

Friends come in all shapes and sizes, but a true friend is one that you really trust—the one who knows how to support you and is honest with you. Someone who lets you make your own choices and doesn't put pressure on you to choose the things they like. Good friends are out there. Try to find them—and keep a little bit of distance between you and anyone who doesn't make you feel good about yourself. This will prevent negative friends from triggering social anxiety.

Peer pressure!

Peer pressure is when you feel as if you have to fit in with your friends or risk being left out in some way. This could happen with clothes and fashion. For example, all of your friends have pierced ears and you don't. It could be with music: all your friends say they like the same band, and you feel you have to like them too.

Peer pressure can also focus on behavior. For example, if all your friends have decided it's okay to be disrespectful to teachers or their parents, you can feel like you have to join in even when you don't want to.

There are other ways that peer pressure can show itself, such as with food and diets, technology and social media, or hobbies and how you spend your free time.

why does peer pressure happen?

Early humans survived more easily in packs or groups, and humans retain a primitive "herd mentality." This may have left us with a habit of looking for things we have in common with other people: if we find other people who are happy to have us around, it makes us feel safer. This habit may be present throughout our lives but may be more obvious in children and young people, especially as they learn to control their emotions and work out who they are. Groups of children will sometimes try to make their group seem "stronger" by all saying they like the same things, and they will try to draw people who like the same things into their group.

Unfortunately, this urge to all share likes and dislikes is difficult for those who think differently or don't like the same things. These people may feel that they will be considered an outsider if they don't try to conform to their peers in some way.

why does this peer pressure cause anxiety?

Peer pressure can cause anxiety because there are always differences between people. Trying to cover these differences up is often difficult. Many people try to belong to groups, but on the inside they can feel as though they don't really belong or that they are likely to be "found out" as different at any moment. They may be afraid that their friends will reject them once they find out that they are actually different.

This causes particular anxiety for kids and young people when they don't really fit into any group, or when they are part of a group but are then rejected by people in the group. This can lead to feeling as if you are "not good enough" or a bad friend. In fact, it might be that you just haven't found the right group of friends.

Easing the peer pressure

It's far too easy to say, **"Just be yourself and everything will turn out okay."** Everyone wants friendships, and being shut out from them is hard. If you find it hard to fit in with everyone, find a group of friends that you do have something in common with, like playing computer games or reading *Harry Potter*, and make the most of it. But while you're doing this, try not to hide the other things about you. You can be a unique individual and part of a group if you go about it the right way.

Also, if you are feeling afraid to dip your toe in a friendship group, start small. Make one friend in the group and work your way through the rest. There are always kind and fun people around who will open up to you. You just have to spot them. Also remember this little phrase: **"To have a friend you must be a friend."** Everyone has their feelings of insecurity.

Being a friend by making other people feel secure
and welcome is a great way to build a strong and
supportive friend group.

social media

Many experts think that the use of technology—social media in particular—is having a big impact on young people, and that it may be responsible for an increase in anxiety among kids.

Social media has moved peer pressure from something that happens mostly at school into every moment of the day. If you are on social media, then people from your peer group can contact you wherever you are. If you find they have been chatting and you haven't seen the messages, you may feel left out. This leads to an urge to constantly check for messages. If something happens to get in the way of checking messages, like a family event, your friends may just continue on without you, and this might make you feel left out. Feeling as if you are being left out of your social group— even when you're not—could trigger some feelings of anxiety about your friends.

Another anxiety-making effect of social media is the feeling that everyone else's life is better than yours—but this isn't true. Some people nickname Facebook as "Fakebook," and for good reason. Anyone can highlight and pick and choose the most exciting and beautiful moments from their lives—leaving out the boring parts and the parts they don't want anyone to see. What people put on social media might be sort of true, but it's not the whole truth.

Social media also gives opportunities for bullies and mean people to tease people (from a "safe" distance) and call them names. This can be a cause of serious anxiety. If you are being bullied online, tell a teacher or another adult you trust, and block anyone who keeps bothering you.

Remember! Keep some perspective.

Try to keep some sense of perspective over what is really important:
friends, family, laughter, life.

Social media is definitely here to stay. Don't ignore it, but don't be a slave to it either. Put your phone away sometimes. You might find that you don't miss it as much as you thought you would. In any case, spending too much time online and not enough with the people who are really around you can lead to anxiety and prevent you from enjoying your life.

We all need balance.

Phones and screens—the effects on your brain

Research is starting to appear about how using phones and tablets affects your brain. Not everything is known yet, but early evidence suggests that using a smartphone for more than four hours each day could lead to an increase in feelings of depression and loneliness. Also, the sleep loss that results from excessive screen use can result in further health and mental health problems.

The effects of screen use on your brain fall into two different areas: the **physical** effects and the **psychological** effects. Both of these could potentially lead toward anxiety.

Media and excessive use of screens can have a bad effect on your sleep. If your phone hums with messages all night, you might not get enough sleep. Screen use has also been linked to difficulties with insomnia, because the light that radiates from the screen prevents your brain from powering down at the end of the day. An hour of no-screen time is recommended before you go to sleep, but plenty of people ignore this advice.

Poor sleep is related to health problems such as heart disease, diabetes, and obesity, but poor sleep is also thought to cause cognitive problems. Your brain doesn't work as well when it's exhausted. This loss of cognitive ability may lead to poor performance in school and even make it more difficult to make important day-to-day decisions.

Other problems of screen and social media use are psychological. Social media users can become addicted to checking their screens and can feel anxious when their devices are unavailable. Some people who use screens a lot may also begin to detach themselves from regular social situations and conversations, and they could begin to feel isolated and alone without really understanding how it has happened.

Some research has considered whether the constant flow of "perfect" faces and bodies on social media may be a cause of anxiety related to poor body image and eating disorders, such as anorexia and bulimia, in teenagers. Studies show that cutting your social media time down to just 30 minutes a day will improve your mental health.

CHAPTER 4
WHAT EFFECT IS ANXIETY HAVING ON YOUR LIFE?

Are you anxious or not?

So, if you think you are anxious, how can you find out?

There are a few questions you need to ask yourself.

How often are you anxious?

How much time do you spend feeling worried or anxious? Is it just occasionally? Is it most of the time? Is it during the day, or does it stop you from sleeping at night?

Keep a diary for a few days and write down the times and places that you feel anxious. If possible, note what you think the reason for the anxiety is. Then go back over the diary. How often were you anxious? How much of your day was spent feeling anxiety? More or less than you guessed? More than you would like?

If you feel you have marked a lot of anxious incidents in the diary, you may need to take some action to deal with your anxiety.

How intense is your anxiety?

This one is tricky to measure, but give it a try. First, draw a straight line. Then, write numbers one through ten along the top of the line.

Now, think about the last time you were really anxious. How would your anxiety score on a scale of one to ten? Was it a really bad ten? Was it a medium-bad five? Or a not-so-bad one? Was it almost more than you could bear, or was it just a little bit of a distraction?

If you feel that the anxiety was almost more than you could bear, you may need to take some action to deal with your anxiety.

what are your symptoms?

When you are anxious, what actually happens to your body? Do you get sweaty and hot? Do you want to cry? Does anxiety stop you from sleeping? Does your pulse race or do you feel panicky? Does your anxiety distract you from whatever task you are doing, or make it difficult for you to complete anything? Does it affect your mood?

If you feel a few of these symptoms, you may need to take some action to deal with your anxiety.

How is anxiety affecting you?

Have you altered your behavior in the long term because of your anxiety? For example, if your anxiety is about friends and going out, do you go out less? If you have a fear of flying, have you started refusing to get on planes?

If you worry a lot about school, is your anxiety causing you to do poorly in class or to avoid school activities? If anxiety has a long-term effect on your life, you may need to seek advice and help.

The next step?

There is no right or wrong answer to any of these questions. They're just to help you understand your own level of anxiety and whether or not it's a problem for you. Everyone feels anxious sometimes, so some anxiety is normal. Finding out how much anxiety you feel, and what is happening to your body when you are anxious, can really help you know how to deal with it.

Try to be as honest as you can in your answers. The more truthful you are, the easier it will be to help yourself.

The role of anxiety in your life

Remember that a small amount of anxiety is okay. In fact, a small amount of anxiety is necessary to protect you from danger, but too much anxiety can start to have a negative effect on your life.

This is a short list of how you can be affected by anxiety. After this, we will explore each one in more detail.

Friends and going out

Anxiety might cause you problems when you want to go out. If you feel anxious about social situations or about meeting new people, then how can you spot this and what can you do about it? In the long term, not dealing with the problem could mean that you miss out on exciting social opportunities.

Family

Anxiety can make you shy, withdrawn, and sometimes bad-tempered. Over a long period of time, this could affect your family relationships.

school

Anxiety could cause problems with your schoolwork. This might be because you are too afraid of failing or too determined to succeed. Or it might be because the physical effects of anxiety, such as sleeplessness, difficulty in concentrating, and restlessness, prevent you from working as effectively as you would like.

sports and hobbies

If your anxiety makes you feel self-conscious, then you might start missing out on activities you enjoy. If you're not comfortable dealing with setbacks in your performance and confronting them in a positive way, you may not be able to reach your full potential.

Health

Anxiety is a mental health problem, and serious anxiety may mean that you stop looking after yourself properly, both physically and mentally. Sometimes anxiety is associated with a wider range of health problems. Learn how to spot this and stop it before it gets serious.

FRIENDS AND GOING OUT

Most people have felt shy at some point in their lives. It normally happens when meeting a lot of new people all at once, like if you start a new school or join a new club. It might happen when you go to a party and you don't know many people.

Social anxiety is a type of anxiety related to being around other people. Some people might think that this is just "being shy," but social anxiety can be more extreme than that. For some people, this occasional feeling of anxiety in new situations can become much more common. You might start to feel social anxiety even around people you know well, such as friends you've known for a long time. This can cause serious problems. For example, you might end up doing activities you don't want to do because you are afraid to say no, or you might end up not getting to do things you love because you are afraid to participate.

Sometimes, social anxiety can make it seem as if you have nothing to say: you get labeled as "quiet." But being shy doesn't mean you don't want to say something—you just feel as if you *can't*.

In the long term, social anxiety may lead to other problems. You might have fewer friends because you don't go out much. You may avoid school trips that could lead to new hobbies and interests. Facing up to situations like applying to college or getting a job might be more stressful than they should be.

To enjoy your place in the world, it is important not to let anxiety about being around other people take over.

Here are some suggestions:

- Don't blame yourself—it's not your fault.

- Role-play being confident. Sometimes pretending to feel confident until you get the hang of it will lead to genuine confidence.

- Focus on being yourself with the people you trust the most.

- Think, "What is the best thing that can happen?" if you are going into a new social situation (or even a familiar one).

- Don't get into the habit of thinking, "I'm just a shy, quiet person, so it's okay to stay in." It's okay to be shy, but at the same time, everyone needs some friends, and everyone has a voice that they need to share with someone. Sometimes you have to give yourself a push and get out there.

If you can't act on any of the ideas above, talking with a counselor or therapist might help you take the steps you need to feel confident and enjoy your time with others.

FAMILY RELATIONSHIPS

The effects of anxiety may be felt in your family. Just as your anxiety may be difficult for you to handle, it may be upsetting for those around you.

If you feel any kind of anxiety in a big way, whether it's an extreme phobia, a fear of going to school, or frequent panic attacks, these may be very difficult for those around you to know how to handle—however much they love you and want to help.

In the early stages of anxiety, you may not realize that there is anything unusual about your behavior, and those around you may just think you are going through a phase if you behave in an angry way or hide away in your bedroom. They may just give you space to work it out yourself.

If your anxiety doesn't go away, however, people will start to notice and will probably make signs that they are trying to help you. This might come in the form of asking if you want to talk, offering to help you with homework, or even offering you small treats or gifts to "make you feel better."

This might feel like the last thing you want if you are not ready to admit that you're not feeling your best. Your family's efforts to make you feel good might feel really invasive. When people love you, unfortunately they don't always know what to do. They don't always know how to solve your problem, but they will help if they can.

Here are some suggestions:

- If you can, take a deep breath and tell a family member what's bothering you. Whether it's panic attacks, fear of going out, or anything else, try to be honest and specific. The more open you are, the more your loved ones can help you.

- If you find it hard to start a conversation about what's worrying you, try to start it when the person you want to talk to is doing something else, like when they're cooking or driving. The distraction might make the conversation easier to start. However, try not to start the conversation when the person you're talking to is also stressed or in a bad mood.

- If starting a conversation is still too difficult, try writing a letter or email instead, including suggestions of what you think could be helpful from the person you're writing to.

- Try to be real. Don't make a joke out of it.

- Be forgiving. Unless the person you are talking to is a trained therapist, they probably won't know what to say, and they are likely to say the wrong thing. Give them time. Most people get better at helping when they have had time to think about what you're telling them.

If you still need to talk to someone outside your family, you could try to talk to a teacher about what is worrying you.

SCHOOL AND STUDY

School can be a lot of fun, but if you struggle with anxiety, school can be difficult too. For some people, school can be a really stressful place.

You may worry about a whole lot of things at school: homework, tests, bullies, teachers, getting teased, doing well in sports or music, or what you're wearing, and whether you fit in. But what effect will these worries have on you in the long term?

For a start, if you feel anxious in school, it can make concentrating really difficult. If you ever have that feeling where you drift off and think about something else after a couple of minutes in the classroom, perhaps something is bothering you. Being distracted means that you won't work as successfully, and that you might not achieve all that you're capable of.

Being anxious about the other kids in school might also prevent you from making friends and finding a supportive community. You may want to make friends with others but feel too anxious about the way they will react to you.

Here are some suggestions:

- Identify one thing about school you enjoy, and focus on that. Even if it's a cookie you have at lunch, it will give you something to look forward to every day.

- You might need to give yourself a little push sometimes to take part in things in the classroom: put up your hand and answer questions and volunteer for classroom jobs. This should make you feel a bit more confident.

- If you worry about schoolwork, tell your teacher or the school counselor. It is their job to help you learn and be your best in school!

- As for other kids, if you take part when people ask you to join in, you will make some friends. Not everyone will be nice to you all the time, but that's their problem—not yours.

SPORTS AND HOBBIES

A happy life has lots of ingredients—it's not all work and studying, family and friends. It's great to have a passion that's just for you, a thing that makes you you. Whatever it is, whether it's martial arts or flower arranging, you have to find it for yourself.

If you suffer from anxiety, however, you might find this more difficult. For a start, if your head is always spinning around the latest thing that's bothering you, you may not feel able to enjoy very much at all. Constant worrying can make it really hard to enjoy yourself. That might mean that when you try a hobby, a craft, or a new sport, you're not really sure whether you like it or not.

Here are some suggestions:

- If you suffer from serious anxiety, some exercise really could be for you. Going for a run, taking up a sport, or doing a class like yoga can release endorphins into your blood that will reduce your anxiety. It will also help you to sleep if you worry at night.

- Making something beautiful, whether it's a cake or a painting, can give you a huge sense of achievement and make you feel proud of yourself, which will raise your self-esteem and may reduce some of your anxiety.

- Singing or playing an instrument in a band is one of the most relaxing things you can do. Along with doing something rewarding, you will also be mixing with people who share the same interests as you.

What good is a hobby, anyway? Well, quite a lot, actually. Hobbies and relaxing pastimes are things that really help us to unwind and deal with anxiety. Some people relax by going for a run, some people relax by playing the piano, and some people relax by painting pictures or cooking. These things help you to focus your mind and concentrate on something that gives you enjoyment—driving away negative thoughts and worry.

HEALTH: THE GUT-BRAIN AXIS

At its most serious, anxiety can start to affect you in physical ways.

The Gut-Brain Axis

Okay, science and gross-out alert all in one here. When you are anxious, do you have stomachaches or cramps or need to use the bathroom a lot? Believe it or not, there are certain internal problems—like irritable bowel syndrome—that can be made worse by anxiety and stress.

The **Gut-Brain Axis** is a real thing that exists in your body. It describes the way that your mood (via your central nervous system) and the bacteria in your gut interact with each other.

Here's how it works. Your brain contains **neurons**, which tell the body how to behave. The gut also has neurons! The neurons in the brain and the gut communicate through the **vagus nerve**, which connects the brain and the gut.

When you are mentally distressed (like when you are anxious), the communication between the brain and the gut is affected. Anxiety has been shown to be a factor in many people with chronic gastrointestinal disorders.

Neurotransmitters

Both the gut and brain also produce neurotransmitters. One common neurotransmitter is serotonin, a lot of which is produced in the gut.

When your brain suffers anxiety, it affects the movement of all neurotransmitters, so feelings such as anxiety are also felt in the stomach.

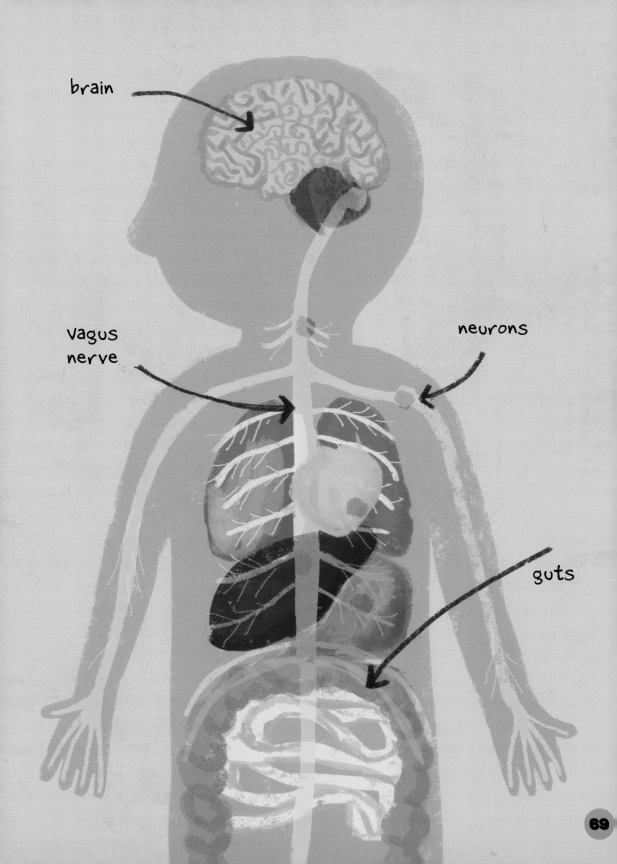

brain

vagus
nerve

neurons

guts

69

Anxiety can also lead to other health issues:

Feeling tearful,
tired, or wobbly

Aches and pains in
your body
– Especially if you aren't
able to relax, so your
shoulders and back get
tense and tight

Loss of appetite
and not eating
enough, or wanting
to eat too much

serious headaches
or migraines

Difficulty with
sleeping at night,
then feeling tired
all day

some skin problems
like itchy skin

Top Tips!

Here are some suggestions to
try to reduce some of these
health issues.

In the next chapter we're going
to look at some methods to calm
yourself so you won't suffer these
physical effects so much. Have a
look at some of those methods
and give them a try.

If there is an activity (say,
swimming or baseball at school)
that makes you particularly
anxious, tell a parent or a teacher.
They should have some advice to
help you.

Remember that these physical
signs are a warning that there is
something you need to sort out or
change. Once you work out what
the problem is, you are on the
road to putting it right, and the
feelings will start to go away..

These can all make life more difficult and need dealing with
quickly. If you start to feel like this, you need to tell an adult,
whether it's someone at school or at home.

CHAPTER 5
TAKING CONTROL
Channeling Your Inner Zookeeper

Remember Fred, the zookeeper we met earlier in the book? To keep the animals quiet, he gave them what they needed: space, peace, time, nourishment, or entertainment.

What can you give to yourself that will calm and nourish your "inner zoo"?

This chapter is a taking-control toolkit. Here, we will explore some of the different ways to make life less anxious and to keep serious anxiety away, leaving your inner zoo animals free to enjoy life in peace and comfort.

Some things in this chapter, like relaxation techniques, are things you can do by yourself.

Other ideas are for ways you might be able to talk to other people, and who you should try to talk to.

Finally, there are some names of some places you can go to for help or information. Not all of these might be relevant to you, but there might be some interesting things for you to read about.

Let's get started!

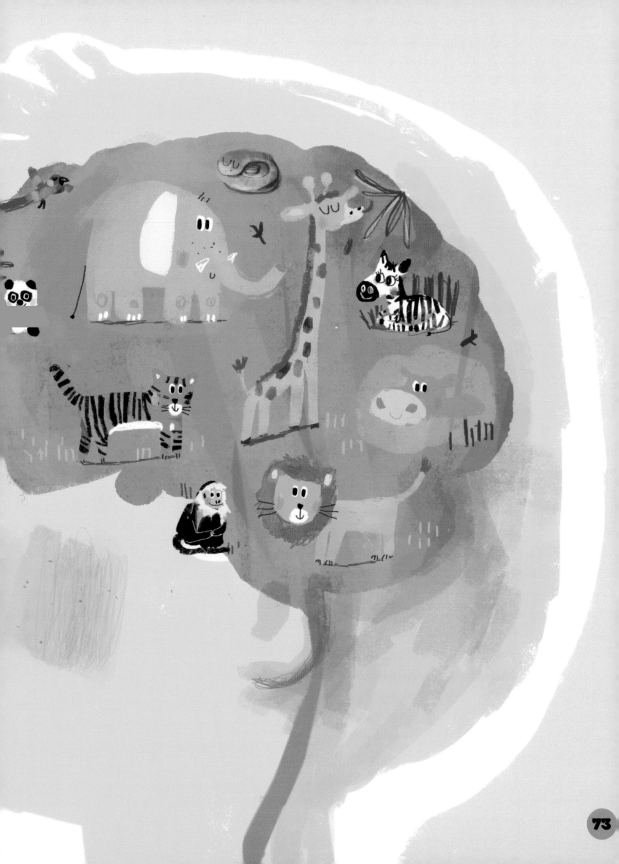

Taking control with your breathing

Have you ever noticed that when you are anxious you start to breathe more quickly, and that this can start to make you feel tingly or a bit light-headed? This is because your body is preparing for "fight or flight"—the prehistoric defense mechanism that we talked about earlier.

When you start to breathe quickly, your body is getting ready to run away from the thing it's anxious about by expelling lots of carbon dioxide and taking in lots of oxygen. In a real-life danger situation, this would help if you needed to run away quickly. Your heart also starts to beat faster and move blood through your veins more quickly. It's not dangerous—it just feels a bit weird. And it can make things like schoolwork or sports a bit harder because your head feels scrambled.

Is this something that happens to you? Next time you find yourself breathing a little too fast, try this.

Find a quiet place—somewhere you feel comfortable.

Close your eyes.

Imagine there's a balloon in your chest.

Breathe in slowly through your nose and picture yourself filling the balloon. Try silently counting to four as you do so.

Hold your breath as you count to four again.

Then breathe slowly out again as you count to four one more time, until the balloon is empty and flopping around.

Do this for about five minutes—or more if you need more time to calm yourself down!

You should feel your head clear and your heart rate slow down. If you do this often, your body will spend more time feeling calm and you will find it easier to deal with your day.

Picturing it better

Visualization is a technique that top athletes use to help them relax before competing. Even if you're not an athlete, you can use visualization to help you stay calm.

Finding your favorite place

Sit or lie down with your eyes closed. Imagine you are in a place that is familiar to you—somewhere you really like. Think about why you like the place. Then, as if you are really there, explore the place with your senses. What can you feel? What can you hear? What can you smell? Is it hot or cold? Can you feel the wind or the sun on your skin? After you have enjoyed your favorite place for a while, gently open your eyes.

Hopefully you will feel more calm and clear-headed.

Filled with your favorite color

**Lie down somewhere quiet and comfortable.
Then think of your favorite color.**

Close your eyes and breathe in deeply. Imagine that the air you breathe is your favorite color. Picture the colored air as it flows into your nose, through your head, and into your chest. On your next breath, picture the color flowing farther through your body, into your stomach and abdomen, and out into your shoulders. On the next breath, picture the color flowing into your arms and legs until you have breathed the color all the way to your fingers and toes. Enjoy the feeling of being full of your favorite color. Imagine you can feel it as you wriggle your fingers and toes. Then, slowly breathe the color back out, starting from your toes, until you are just you again.

Picturing a positive outcome

When you are worried about a particular situation, it can help to picture the situation ending well.

For example, if you are worried about taking a test, close your eyes and picture the day of the test. Start when you are standing outside the classroom. Then walk into the room and sit at your desk. Take out your pen. When it's time to turn over the paper, you calmly read through the questions and answer them as well as you can, leaving time to check over your answers at the end.

Or if you are worried about a social situation, picture yourself enjoying that situation.

First, decide what you will be wearing. Will you be in fancy clothes or casual clothes? What clothes make you feel your best? Picture yourself in those. Then, imagine that you are walking into the party. You see your friends and go talk to them. Think about what you could talk about. Finally, picture yourself laughing and eventually waving to everyone and heading home, having had a good time.

RELAXING YOUR MUSCLES

muscle relaxing

Another way to "trick" your body calm is to relax all your muscles. To do this, first you have to make them tense!

Lie down somewhere quiet. (You can do this to help you sleep as well.) Starting with your face, scrunch up all the muscles in your eyes, and then relax them. Then wrinkle your nose as if you've gotten too close to Dad's socks, and relax again. Then twist up your mouth as if you've eaten something sour, and then relax.

Moving on, try to touch your ears with the tips of your shoulders, and then let them down again. Keep on like this all the way down your body until each set of muscles has had a turn. Your body should feel more relaxed and ready to rest.

Body scan

A body scan is a good, slow way to spend some time with yourself and really deal with any hidden feelings of anxiety.

Lie down somewhere quiet and comfortable without too many distractions. Gently focus your mind on your body and how it feels. There are all sorts of little sensations—tingles, aches, your own pulse—which we're normally too busy to notice. Try to focus on these in the stillness and think about how they feel.

If you find it hard to get started, you could be systematic about it. Start at your head and see what you feel, then gradually work down through the rest of your body.

No one ever really manages to concentrate perfectly on this kind of activity to start with, so don't beat yourself up if your mind starts to wander. If you notice that you've become distracted in the middle of your body scan, just try to continue where you left off. It's no big deal.

It might take a few tries to get good at doing a body scan, but when you practice it regularly, you will feel in tune with what your body is trying to tell you about your state of mind.

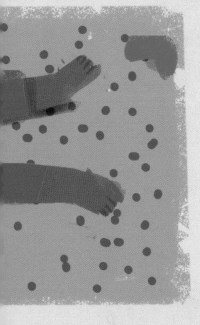

make it up

If you want to, try a combination of deep breathing, muscle relaxing, and visualization. A combination might relax you really well.

WHO TO TALK TO?

When you have anxiety that is affecting your life in a negative way, one of the most important ways to deal with it is talking to someone about it. But who should you talk to? A friend, family member, or trusted adult? Or do you need a professional, like a counselor or therapist? The answer to this question will depend on how anxious you are and how much your anxiety is affecting your life.

If you have a friend or relative who you trust, and who might be able to make you see things from a different perspective, then it's certainly worth talking to them. For example, if you are worried about the way you seem to other people, or if you suffer from some social anxiety, talking to a sympathetic friend might help comfort you and put you at ease.

However, as much as they love you, your family and friends are not experts in how to deal with anxiety. Talk to people in your life, but if your anxiety remains a problem, consider seeing a professional for more help.

Asking a doctor or a counselor for help

The best way to go about getting treatment for your anxiety is to start by asking at your school. They may have regular counselors who work with the school. These people will specialize in your age group and will have seen many similar cases before.

Alternatively, you could talk to your doctor. They should also be able to put you in touch with someone who specializes in helping people your age. Ask your parents or guardians to make an appointment to talk about your anxiety.

If possible, it is best to always keep your family informed about what's going on. If a therapist recommends a particular technique or treatment, it will be really helpful to have your family's support, even if you don't want to tell them everything about what's causing your anxiety.

HOW TO TALK ABOUT ANXIETY: GETTING IT OUT THERE

Starting a conversation about your anxiety might feel like the hardest thing in the world. You may feel afraid of telling others what you're going through, and even after you overcome this fear, it can still be difficult to explain what you're going through to someone else. Try these steps:

- First, try to get the person on their own and at a time when they are not distracted. Tell them that you have something important you'd like to talk about, so that you have their full attention.

- Keep it simple. Say that you think your anxiety is becoming a problem in your life and that you think you might need some help with it.

- Explain to this person that you have chosen them because you feel they will support you in dealing with this problem.

At this point, it is possible that a parent or friend will want to minimize your anxiety by saying something like "It can't really be that bad," or "It's just part of growing up." Stick to your point and make them see that it's more than that, and that you need their help. You can't expect your friends and family to morph into the perfect listener on demand, but that doesn't mean they won't start to understand given time.

Talking to a professional

If you do make an appointment with a counselor or other professional, they may use a particular therapy specifically designed to help with your anxiety. One particular method you might encounter is Cognitive Behavioral Therapy.

Cognitive Behavioral Therapy (or CBT for short)

CBT is a talking-based therapy that can help you manage your problems by changing the way you think and behave. It's based on the idea that your thoughts, feelings, and actions are interconnected and can trap you into a pattern of behavior that doesn't help you. CBT aims to break any negative patterns to improve the way you feel.

In a course of CBT, usually between 5 and 20 weeks, the therapist will help you break down your problems into separate parts and analyze them separately. After each session you go away and try to put into action what you have learned.

Of course, if you are living with an ongoing problem like a sick relative or money worries, CBT can't take that problem away. However, CBT can give you coping strategies to change the way you feel about the problem.

USE YOUR ANXIETY TO MAKE YOU SUPERPOWERED

Anxiety? Bring it on!

This may sound a little strange. We've been talking for almost this whole book about how anxiety can be a bad thing for your life, but now we're going to consider life without it for a few minutes. Because anxiety isn't all bad—sometimes it can be useful.

Yes, in the proper amount, anxiety's not always a bad thing: it's the brain's way of protecting us from danger. And sometimes you can even harness it to help you perform difficult tasks.

Top athletes rely on the rush of energy and increased focus that comes from mild anxiety. They often use visualization to see the different outcomes of their actions. Imagining themselves succeeding or failing is a great incentive for them to focus and put everything into the performance. Musicians and theater actors learn how to harness their nerves to give extra vitality to their performance. And in school, a little bit of stress can motivate you to study extra hard and concentrate on the big exam.

A *small* amount of anxiety is a really good motivator. Without some anxiety, we might not feel inclined to put in so much effort both at school and in our relationships. Imagine if you had no anxiety at all in your friendships. Would you work as hard to be a good friend? Similarly, in school or work, would you always expect to do your best without any anxiety?

In situations that require leadership, experience with anxiety can be a help rather than a hindrance. People who have felt anxious are very good at considering the pros and cons of a situation. Experience with anxiety can also make you good at empathizing with other people who struggle to deal with anxiety in some situations.

If you feel anxiety mostly in pressure situations, try not to fight it but to embrace it. Your feelings of anxiety are part of your nature as a human being, so use them if you can.

Be the boss of your anxiety, rather than letting your anxiety be the boss of you.

DEAL WITH ANXIETY IN A POSITIVE WAY—SOME IDEAS

Keep people around you.

When you feel anxious, it's natural that you might start to spiral downward and into yourself. You might start to stay away from friends and spend ages reading about the way you feel on the internet—or in books like this! Just remember, while understanding your own emotions is important, it's important to escape from yourself and your thoughts as well. Be around your family and friends. Watch movies with other people. Go grocery shopping with your parents. Seek out the people who make you feel good.

Identify the cause of your anxiety. Can you challenge it to a staring contest?

For example, for social anxiety, try to talk to one new person every day, or put up your hand and answer a question every day in class.

Or if you have a phobia about spiders, try to look at a picture online, watch a video on YouTube, and then see a really big one at the zoo!

If you have generalized anxiety, try to do one spontaneous thing every day for a week.

Often, the key to beating anxiety is to show yourself that the thing you're afraid of has less power to hurt you than you think. Showing this to yourself can be really helpful.

Exercise—then exercise some more.

Exercise changes your brain. It increases the activity of dopamine and serotonin in your system. These chemicals contribute to your sense of well-being by making you feel happy and relaxed, combating your feelings of anxiety and making you feel able to cope.

Eat well.

Sorry about this one if you like junk food! Earlier, we talked about the Gut-Brain Axis. Some evidence suggests that eating foods that promote a variety of gut bacteria (such as nuts, whole wheat, and green leafy vegetables) could have a positive effect on your mood. In any case, too many sweets, too much processed food, and caffeine can definitely lower your mood—so watch what you eat.

Laugh!

Believe it or not, laughing is good for you—particularly in dealing with anxiety. The change in brain chemistry that comes with a good belly laugh includes increased blood flow and lower blood pressure, and gives you a burst of energy that makes life seem easier.

YOU ARE NEVER ALONE

If you're not sure where to start, the following are all places that you can look for good advice about your anxiety. But remember, whether you choose to talk to friends, family, your teachers, professional counselors, or your cat, you never need to deal with this alone.

Anxiety Centre: anxietycentre.com

This is an organization dedicated to helping anxiety sufferers deal with their disorder through self-help and treatment. Visit their website for more information.

Psychology Today: psychologytoday.com

This website has articles and information about all aspects of psychology and mental health. Search past articles for information and research on anxiety. It also has a directory of local therapists.

NAMI HelpLine: 1-800-950-6264

The HelpLine of the National Alliance on Mental Illness (NAMI) provides support and referrals to anyone suffering from a mental problem or disorder, including anxiety.

American Academy of Pediatrics: www.aap.org

This medical website has useful information about children's mental health problems and how to get help.

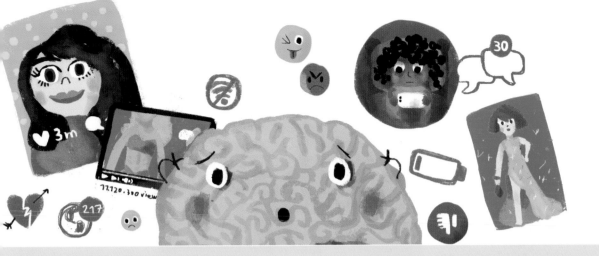

American Acadamy of Child & Adolescent Psychiatry (AACAP)

The mission of AACAP is to promote the healthy development of children, adolescents, and families through advocacy, education, and research, and to meet the professional needs of child and adolescent psychiatrists throughout their careers.

Mental Health America: mhanational.org

Search the site for information about anxiety.

Contributors:

Carrie Lewis has edited and written more than 100 books for children. She has contributed to a wide range of educational resources and has recently become a tutor working in the area of family learning. She is married with two children and plays the cello.

Sophia Touliatou works as an illustrator, doing mostly children's books, many of which have gained merits and awards. You can find her work in Greece, France, Italy, Germany, Spain, the United States, and other countries around the world.

Published in 2020 by Beaming Books, an imprint of 1517 Media. All rights reserved.

No part of this book may be reproduced without the written permission of the publisher. Email copyright@1517.media. Printed in the USA.

26 25 24 23 22 21 20   1 2 3 4 5 6 7 8

ISBN: 978-1-5064-6320-9

Library of Congress Cataloging-in-Publication Data

Names: Lewis, Carrie (Children's author) author. | Touliatou, Sophia,
    illustrator.
Title: All about anxiety / written by Carrie Lewis ; illustrated by Sophia
    Touliatou.
Description: Minneapolis : Beaming Books, 2020. | Audience: Ages 9-13 |
    Summary: "Anxiety. It's an emotion that rears its head almost every day,
    from the normal worries and concerns that most of us experience, to
    outright fear when something scary happens, to the anxiety disorders
    that many kids live with daily. But what causes anxiety? And what can we
    do about it? All About Anxiety tackles these questions from every
    possible angle. Readers will learn what's going on in their brain and
    central nervous system when they feel anxious. They'll learn about the
    evolutionary reasons for fear and anxiety and that anxiety isn't always
    a bad thing--except for when it is! Most importantly, kids will discover
    new strategies to manage their anxiety so they can live and thrive with
    anxiety."-- Provided by publisher.
Identifiers: LCCN 2019042628 | ISBN 9781506463209 (hardcover)
Subjects: LCSH: Anxiety--Juvenile literature. | Anxiety in
    children--Juvenile literature.
Classification: LCC BF575.A6 L49 2020 | DDC 155.4/1246--dc23
LC record available at https://lccn.loc.gov/2019042628

Beaming Books
PO Box 1209
Minneapolis, MN 55440-1209
Beamingbooks.com